FOR THE UNSPEAKABLE

Dear Sheryl,

May you be greatly
blessed in your journey
with the Lord!

A Wondering Soul

Reihana

WORDS FOR THE UNSPEAKABLE

SHARED EMOTIONS -
OVERCOMING CHILDHOOD TRAUMA

RIEKE BUTT

A WONDERING SOUL

DENVER, COLORADO

Words for the Unspeakable
Shared Emotions - Overcoming Childhood Trauma
All Rights Reserved.
Copyright © 2012 Rieke Butt - A Wondering Soul
v2.0

Outskirts Press, Inc.
http://www.outskirtspress.com

ISBN: 978-1-4327-8226-9

Outskirts Press and the "OP" logo are trademarks belonging to Outskirts Press, Inc.

PRINTED IN THE UNITED STATES OF AMERICA

Thanks and Acknowledgements

This book would not have been in existence today and certainly not in published form, had not so many people encouraged me all the way. Planting the seed for the idea to put my writings into a book, so that other people may benefit from expressing myself in writing as well. Checking in, to keep me on track when I felt like giving up. And to constantly remind me that good can come from this, as well as being understanding with this long, but worthwhile process.

The biggest support came all along from my loving husband. He put up with me hiding away, trying to work on myself and finding a way to express myself. Words can not express enough appreciation for such love in action, but THANK YOU.

And also a big thank you to my son, who often tried to listen and understand, I am sure it was not easy at times.

Also to my wonderful councellor from the Sexual Assault Center, Shirley. Other ladies from groups that are dealing with the same or similar issues, some are now very good friends; Co-workers, church members, friends and many more…

To my friend Mindy a big thank you for helping with proof reading some of this material. And to Larry from Outskirtspress, for being patient with me when I was trying to figure out where I wanted to take this project. And this would not be complete without mentioning Helen, as without her, this book would not be in print, or at least not yet. She is one of the most encouraging women I have met so far. And she unselfishly gave time, financial assistance and most of all got me spiritually back on track, when I was ready to have this disappear in the closet again!

And last, but absolutely not least to God and Jesus, for being there, every step of the way. Even when I had my back turned to his love and understanding. And for giving me the opportunity to heal and share my pain, fears and hope with other survivors this way.

The ability to express my feelings in words, connecting this way to others, stopping the loneliness after so many years through sharing.

My prayer is that this book will bring consolation to others going through this painful experience. May this be encouragement and a sign that you are also not alone in this journey of healing!

Contents

Poems

Introduction

This book started out as a collection of written emotions that I collected over the years in my journey to process and overcome the consequences of childhood abuse. It is a way for me to address the feelings inside, take them out of me and keep them in a safe place to revisit them when needed. It helps me to get free on the inside of these sometimes negative and damaging, but very real feelings. By letting go of them slowly, it creates room on the inside for positive, healing and happy feelings. It is very important for me though to be able to work some more on these issues when I feel strong enough and ready to deal with them, a bit at a time. Having them safe in written form, I can connect to the events in the past by reading up on them. It used to take so much energy to repress all those unpleasant memories and feelings. I struggled with what was left to make it through the day and could not understand why I was always so easily exhausted.

Now I can use some of that energy to process and heal instead. But it is more than a tool for myself. I eventually entrusted some special people with what I had written, feeling I am putting my darkest secrets out there. I was surprised how people reacted. They did not correct me, or made fun of me, but rather encouraged me to put this out there. Somehow they found a new way to connect to the real me inside and this was a totally new experience. I got hope out of that and was getting myself ready to let the truth of the past come out, no more running and hiding from the past. It does take a lot of courage to stand up and stop running from those shadows, but it also takes the control away from the abuse and the abuser itself. Once you open up, you are no longer held captive by the old secrets.

It started out as a form of journaling for me, but by the grace of God, I hope this to be a helpful tool for others facing the same experiences. Or for people who want to understand loved ones going through this. There are way too many people, men and women, that are living with the memories of this ugly past today. Statistics claim that one in three people experience sexual abuse at some point in their life.

So if you are willing to see, there are people right around you, that are affected by this kind of past.

The year 2009 was a very important and eventful year and I am not surprised anymore that I also started the process for publishing this book. Because of other events in my life I started to open up to God and He started to work in my heart and my mind. Helped me to clean up on the inside with fire and gave me the strength to let go of anger and hurt feelings towards people in my life. He truly renews us from the insie out, if we let Him! When I asked God why He left me when I was hurting so much, He told me that He never did, but I was the one to scared to trust Him. And He also gave me my best friend, my husband. So that I would not have to face all this alone and simply hold me when needed. He connected me to the right people, guiding me through the Holy Spirit and told me He can only work in my heart once I started to trust Him and started to open up to Him. You see, all those years when I felt alone, He was waiting for me to accept His invitation. And once I started to slowly let Him take control and just accepted, things started to happen in my life. He does give me messages through altered quotes of the bible. I will give one example here of one that I was given in the beginning and it is what inspired me and gave me the courage to publish his book.

I am talking about my version of *Isaiah 52*.

I believe it applies to all of us in one way or another. But if it touches you in some way, it is probably also a message for you!

I was very fortunate to have the opportunity to be baptized again as an adult. And I took this as an opportunity to die to my old, hurt and troubled way of life. God has given me not only hope, but also a chance to have new life in him right now. Not just after physical death. I can start to see things from a different perspective and the old hurts and wounds are still real, but they are turning into opportunities for blessings.

If he allows me to use this pain transformed to understanding and a way to bring hope to others, then this journey is well worth it. I am still a survivor today and will still have to deal with memories of the past, lies I have been told and struggles that this kind of past will bring. But I am much more hopeful today and I know now there is hope through Christ. As he takes us broken and wounded and loves us just the same!

It took a lot of praying and willpower to forgive the people that willingly or unconsciously have hurt me in the past. But I needed to forgive them for my own sanity's sake. And ever since I did, with the help of the Holy Spirit, I feel like I am finally moving forward. I have hope for the future and am a much happier person than I thought I was capable of being. I am thankful now to be alive and I can enjoy it, rather than seeing life itself as a punishment and agonizing.

There is hope, so keep looking for it and don't give up…

God loves you just as you are!

Please be respectful of what is being shared here. Do not try to judge, but rather just try to open up and try to understand and connect to what is being expressed here.

My Isaiah 52

*Get up out of the dirt
and make a move.
You have been captive by
unbelief long enough.
Get out of the pit of despair.
You have been in evils captivity
long enough now. I will deliver
you without money,
but by the blood of Christ!*

1

A Summary of My Background

When I started with this project I was going to just list my poems and so express feelings that I have had, or still have at times. And so you can see the changes that happened over time in the written words. But the more I was working with my own feelings, writing and processing, the more it seemed to make sense to give a bit more background information on myself and my situation. I do not mean to give a biography and certainly do not want to make this about me as a person. But it became clear that it was easier for people to relate to what I was expressing in my writings, when they had a bit of the history to go with it. Well, as much as I can remember it. And if other people of my family were asked, they may have a different way of remembering it, as it affected them different. But this is what I can recollect and what feelings I have memorized.

I was born in the late sixties in western Canada, to parents that were from two completely different worlds. My mother a catholic raised European and a father that comes from a Muslim Asian background. That is where different values and beliefs are starting to get confusing for a child. As one pretty much has to learn to stay flexible and compromise constantly.

When I was still under school age my parents moved to Germany and I had to adjust to a completely different environment and language. My parents still struggled in their marriage and I witnessed verbal and physical abuse even then. One day my father disappeared and my mother filed for divorce. It seemed like only month after, when we moved in with a new family. My mother was to replace the mother to my new stepfather's children. His wife passed away after giving birth to the fourth child. So a stepbrother, three stepsisters and his mother in law (of his first wife) living in the same household. Still grieving the loss of her daughter, their grandmother struggled to accept the new family dynamics and of course my mother and me. I mostly remember the daily torments of being told that I did not belong there. And in the beginning she asked my mother when we would leave again.

My stepfather buried himself in work and when

not working overtime at one of his two jobs, would go and get drunk to avoid reality. I remember I was told to be grateful and happy that "someone took me in" and paid for what I needed. I used every opportunity not having to be at home, stayed as much as possible with my maternal grandmother, or just found other excuses not having to be there. My grandmothers second husband was very controlling, emotional abusive and made her life a "living hell", but I was used to that and at least I wasn`t told constantly that I did not belong there. She made me feel like at least one person cared for me and when she passed away when I was 13, I took this very hard and felt I had no one in this world left.

I eventually found other places to "hide out at" and stayed in the city, visited people we hardly knew or went to the horse market. Being around animals was very important to me, as they showed me unconditional love, which I hardly knew from family.

I only felt safe in my room with the door locked and I played the music so loud that I couldn`t hear the hurtful things resounding in my head. And feeling the music in my stomach distracted me from the nausea I often felt. I didn`t realize of course this wasn`t normal and I was told by my mother that I must have inherited a mental disease through the inter-marriages on my dad`s side of the family. Of course this is not actually possible. And I had questioned several mental health professionals, before I started to let go of that lie. Psychiatrists and other therapists have affirmed me that all the depression and anxiety are really a result of the early abandonment and abuse. "A so called normal reaction, to un-normal circumstances". And it has actually resulted in what is known today as *post traumatic stress syndrome.*

So Numb

*Does being numb mean I am dumb? You told me to be
quiet and take it. You said no one wants to know. Those
feelings are mine and don`t belong in the open. So what
should I do? I take them and swallow, just stuff them in. As
only "good girls" are allowed in. I try and fit in, but only as
long as I know where my place is… quiet and strong. On
the inside I have to confess, oh dear what a mess.*

*You made sure I will stay quiet, but only god knows I
am getting tired. The feelings are going to some place
unknown. Along they take the smiles and the laughter.
And than you wonder what is coming after.*

*I tell you now feeling numb, by all means is being dumb. If
anything, I have to say, those people that said be quiet and
take it, should walk in your shoes and feel what you feel.*

*Not dumb and worthless, but kind, smart and good.
They took this away from us, make us feel like we don`t
belong. But it is them that should feel dumb and really
not strong. So if you feel numb, just like I, take a deep
breath and remember why. It was them that took our
feelings away and this is really not okay!*

2

The Start of Awareness

Starting to realize what it means to be an abused person is overwhelming and scary. Somehow you always know, but there is nothing concrete. It is almost harder when the memories are not conscious yet, as we still react to things we see, smell and/or hear. But since the link to the past experience is still not there, we think we are crazy. Something does not seem to fit and the norm does not seem normal for a person with abuse in the past. By the way, what is normal? A friend of mine says: "The setting on the dryer!" Is normal not really a measure that a person uses based on their values and what they were taught growing up?! So really everybody has a little bit of a different "normal".

But back to realizing there is an unpleasant history…
For me it was often very confusing when my husband and I were watching a movie and somehow in the

middle of it, I completely changed how I felt and often even more changed how I behaved. I would suddenly get distant, left the room and started crying for no obvious reason, so I thought. The more my husband wanted an answer on what was wrong and how he could help, the more frightened I felt and I was even less able to answer him, shutting down. It felt like I was a hurt, wild animal trapped inside a cage and his questioning was like provoking the animal from the outside of the cage. Making the space on the inside smaller and smaller. I remember like feeling climbing up the wall, as there was nowhere else left to go. I could not piece these things together at first. My husband didn`t understand either and was getting frustrated, feeling left out. It is like a viscous cycle, where a relationship or the individual can suffer greatly. And so often marriages will not survive the consequences, unless good counseling is available and accessible.

We started to notice after some time that it was usually after some force, like a rape, or a not so obvious controlling relationship in a movie, or other things we watched and/or just discussed. I knew I was sensitive when it came to relationships with men and viewed them pretty much all as controlling and violent. It took a lot of years to learn that in reality not all men are alike and that even women can be the aggressive, abusive partner in the relationship. I also never wanted to be married and had great conflicts to go through with our wedding. Even though I did not doubt the feelings for my husband. I cried in my wedding night, still thinking I made the greatest mistake by now "being owned" by my husband. There is a saying in my father`s culture that might explain my feelings… "One day you are your fathers property, the next day you are your husband`s property" (in reference to a wedding).

But I am not trying to single out one culture here and make them look like the only ones responsible. Looking back in European history, men there also put a woman's value in a serving role and of a lower status as men as well. Men from that society are just as controlling and it is socially accepted in general. I think only in this generation have we started to slowly change our views on what an abusive relationship is and that men or women, do not have the right to control and dominate their partner in any type or form. If I take a look back to the relationships of my mother, my mother in law and the one of my grandmother, I can see changes happening for the better. In the past there was no true opportunity to leave a controlling, even abusive spouse for a woman. Especially if there are children involved. I remember my grandma`s way of thinking: "You made your bed, now sleep in it!". To her there was no other option, as to somehow survive and live with the daily terror. And she used to get up in the mornings, barely awake, crying already over insults she had to take before she was even out of bed. Till today I have no idea, other than her prayers, how she managed to live through all the hurt.

Sometimes I forget to thank god for putting me in a time and place where I am free to choose to stay in a relationship or leave. By all means, I am not making divorce the answer to a non functioning relationship. I truly believe that everything possible should be attempted first to restore a relationship. And I am aware that it takes constant hard work to make a relationship work. But if the partner is not able to see his/her hurtful behavior as such and was never taught any different, leaving him/her unwilling to change, it is extremely difficult to resolve issues. In some cases marriage counseling can be quite effective, but finding the right match in a councilor is a complicated process in itself. I will not judge anyone that feels no longer safe with their partner and feels like they need to leave in order to have a life. We are thankfully a society here in Canada where people are free to do what keeps them safe, physically and emotionally. Having a justice system that slowly starts to recognize what abuse is and is working towards better protecting people. But our society still has a long way to go yet and we as a society need to get past all the myth that are out there.

We all know it takes two people to make a marriage work and I wonder sometimes how unprepared people enter into a marriage without realizing the consequence of an un-committed relationship? But this leads to a whole new topic and I am leaving this part open to everyone`s personal interpretation.

Responsibility of Men

Why am I so angry?
There is nothing I can do.
It strips me of my power,
controls my every move.
I do not want to feel like this.
What makes it go away?
This very little book of mine
might tell me what`s the way.
who gave men this power?
Who TOLD them this is right?
I am a person also and wanted to decide,
want to control my very own life.
But I can only do so, if they will let me go.
Men have to learn a lesson,
a lesson in compassion.
And I can only hope,
this will come true one day,
all over the whole world.

I think it is safe to say that after abuse, especially when it occurs early on in life, the relationship with oneself is actually hurting. We get taught that our needs do not matter, or that we have to put others first. We lose the connection to our inner-self. If the emotional pain is severe, a safety response is triggered for protection that is called "disassociating". It allows for a temporary disconnection of the mind from the body and during this time no conscious memory is formed. People that have abuse in their past are probably aware of what I am talking about. For others, imagine it like an emotional coma. When you "come back", there is no clear awareness of what took place. Some people still sense that something awful happened, but are not sure in fact as to what, and often it is to scary to actually find out.

Professionals also talk about the "inner child". Because of the trauma that takes place when a person is still developing on an emotional level, normal behavior patterns get disrupted and the so called inner child stays at that stage and does not really grow up. While on the outside we learn to cope and cover up what people do not want to see, everything appears to be ok. Only things do not add up and we have no memory and connection to what is going on at the subconscious level. And how could it, crying because of feeling sad, showing fear or asking for a hug because we need to feel loved, is usually not accepted behavior in an abusive environment. "Suck it up", or "Don`t be such a baby, I can give you a reason to cry" is much more likely to be heard, than loving, caring words that could make a world of difference. We tend to continue with negative self-talk and will run ourselves down, so that the abuser does not have to anymore. This is why survivors often believe the abuser that we actually deserve what happened. Even worse the abuser will often use threats to keep the victim from speaking up and with that take away what belongs to the victim: sanity and safety! Shame and fear will often keep victims from confronting an abuser and so it takes a long time to change from a victim to a survivor. Living in and with the secret is what keeps us from connecting to other people around us and an emotional isolation is one of the major consequences of childhood abuse. So many try to compensate with addictions, self-hurting, eating disorders and a suicidal lifestyle and thoughts. It is a vicious cycle that keeps a lot of survivors trapped, not functioning to societies standards and often living with severe depression.

3

My Story…

I like to start with one very early memory that is vague, but also still disturbing when it comes up in dreams. I am not sure exactly at what age this was, but it was shortly after moving to Germany. My parents were fighting and I do not know, or at least don't remember why. But my dad suddenly lost control and took a wooden hockey stick and started beating my mother over the head sitting in a big chair across from me in the living room. My dad, who I usually loved, looked suddenly so scary, bigger and not safe at all. He seemed to turn into a raging "monster" and did not look like my parent, a person that a child depends on.

When I saw blood running from my mom's forehead and she started to cry, I guess I went into shock. I started screaming, now standing in the doorway, thinking of running, but unsure of where to go. So I froze right there and just screamed and cried. At least it made my dad stop, probably snapping him out of what possessed him, dropped the hockey stick and tried to console me. Telling me he was sorry for scaring me, telling me everything was ok now and asked me to stop crying. I think he was actually shocked himself.

Since I was very young, I am not sure if this is in the right order. But the other thing that happened around that time, was that our neighbor in the next apartment figured out that my father actually was Pakistani and from that day on, I was not allowed to play with her daughter anymore, who was roughly the same age. Up to then, we played with dolls on a blanket between the apartment buildings, or hide and seek with other kids from the neighborhood. All of a sudden their excuse was that I could not even speak the language proper and when her mom seen us in the hallway she looked the other direction as if we did not exist and no more `hello how are you`. It did not make sense to me and I could not figure out what I had done. Maybe my grandmother's husband was right and I was, what he called a "bastard". Not that I really understood the meaning of the word at that age, but by the way everyone now treated me, it must mean I am a person of less value, right?!

Identity was very confusing for me anyway. I was not used to be called by my real, legal name. The German relatives would use my German first name and my dad's friends would call me by my Muslim name. So my mother thought it would be easier to just take the first part of one name and the last part of the other and create a new call name. Later on as an attempt to look like a happy family, my mother convinced the school to address me under my stepfathers last name, without ever being adopted or having a legal name change. So the report cards I have from my elementary school are in a name of a person that does not exist. I had to keep this made up name, since one of the girls in the stepfamily already had my legal name and instead of confusing her, they kept calling me by the made up name. My mom`s latest life partner still gets angry with me when I leave a message on the answering machine under my real, legal name, that I go by today. Not sure why he has any reason to feel affected at all?

It wasn`t until I moved back to Canada that I felt safe enough to use a Muslim name. There are still a lot of people who are very prejudice in Germany. That is likely one of the biggest reasons I always wanted to go back to Canada. Hoping to be treated for who I really am and on how I act, versus by my cultural background.

I witnessed enough people treating others different based on where their parents came from personally, more than once. And to give another example, a boy that was around kindergarten age, adopted from another country and a visible minority, was hung in the playground by other kids, for "not belonging to their views" of a German society. His adoptive mother watched from the balcony of a high-rise apartment, running down to the playground in a panic, only to find her adoptive son dead. It was too late. This is not a made up story, it happened in the 90`s in Bremerhaven, Germany. The shocking part is, it is this new generation of children that is capable of seeing no value in someone else`s life, to feel like it is ok to take that life, simply because that person is different!

It was a big problem throughout history and it will be in the future. We get blinded into believing to be superior and the other party is of less value. But this is the root of all evil. By not being open minded and tolerant of the differences, we treat others unfair and even allow for crimes to take place. That is why I believe one of god`s commandments is to <u>not judge</u>.

Even today there are so many examples it would fill a book by itself. We would have so much to learn from each other if we would be open to it. For example the original way of life of Native American people. To never take more than what is needed and to see us as a part of this wonderful planet, rather than looking at it as an opportunity to plunder it till everything is destroyed, which no doubt will lead to our own destruction. Simply to satisfy the greedy nature of our society and our wish for personal conveniences. And to justify this behavior, we look at other people as less deserving and of less value. That is why we raise a new generation that is capable of committing such horrible crimes. They have learned OUR values…

Why Are We Here

We have to go through life wondering why
all this is happening to us.
Who has all the answers?
Do we already know?
Or is the secret of life this very thing,
to find why we are born?
I would like to know who writes
this book of life?
Did we decide before we came?
All these questions and only little answers.
Just maybe there is light at the end of the road…
But we could use some light now,
to give us the strength to pull through this.
I know I am not alone, yet it feels like it
a lot of times.
And where are all the answers?

Why

I don`t know how to say it?
This does seem so unfair.
So many women crying and
they are in despair.
Their voices are so hard to hear.
Who did this injustice to them
and why do they stay so quiet?
There are so, oh so many.
But who really wants to know?
And what is there to do?
We are all responsible,
because we have our choices.
Have YOU not also heard some voices?
Are you not able to see and hear them?
Wake up now and do your part
and show some kindness and your support!

I Am So Scared

I am so scared and don`t know why.
I see dark shadows more and more.
I am getting tired of fighting them,
they seem to come more often now.

How do I explain these shadows?
What makes them go away?
Who knows what I am talking about?
Will there be light at the end of this road?

I don`t know how to tell him,
but at least he wants to listen.
One day I will find myself,
maybe he`ll understand than too
and everything explains itself.

Continuing with me as a child, more things changed in a hurry. It seems like only a short time between events. But dad was suddenly gone and I was sure I must have been not good enough or not worthy for my dad to care what will happen to me. My mother told me later that I first told her "It` s ok mom, we just buy a new dad…"

She figured I was dealing better with this than she had expected me to, but on the inside I was missing my dad terribly. He had his anger issues, but was also the parent that told me he loved me and held me. I have no recollection of affection from my mother. It was more like I had to be really good around her and watch I would not upset her. I was still under school age when my mother got married again to a widower that had one son and three daughters from a previous marriage. The new stepbrother was five years older, the twins one year older and there was a baby girl that was just about a year old. Their mother had died from bleeding to death after the birth of the last girl. The baby stayed for month in the hospital and than an aunt looked after her, until my mother and I moved into the house. Their maternal grandmother also lived in the same household, still grieving the loss of her daughter. I remember the first day moving in. The twins and I were playing in the yard in pretty new dresses and it was warm and sunny. We were called into the house and I followed the girls to the front door. Their grandmother closed the front door when she seen me coming and before I knew it, I hit my forehead on the heavy door. I started to cry and my mother came looking to see what was going on. When my new stepfather picked me up, his mother in law got really upset and asked how he could pick me up, since I was not his child. Than disregarding that my mother and her son in law were just married, asked her how long she intended to stay and made it clear she did not approve of us at all. The resentment continued and so it felt like treading through a mine field most of the time.

She moved out later on, but by then the stepbrother and the two older stepsisters were well trained by her. And I was daily challenged and made to feel unwelcome. Having the two stepsisters blocking my way, confronting me and only allowing me to pass after teasing me about being an evil stepsister. They repeated almost daily that I was not a part of their family. I often cried out of anger, trying desperately to find a reason and a justification for being alive and simply being there.

While deep down inside I started to believe what I was told by the majority in this family. I was made fun of on how much I ate, the way I dressed and whatever they could find. Today they might tell me it was just *teasing* fun, but given the circumstances and the consistency it was quite real and threatening to me. My mother often didn`t see any of the intimidation and when I tried to talk about it, she would say that I am just to sensitive and that I needed to make this work. Family *oh yeah* was needed later on in life! So I just did not bother her anymore with feeling frightened. It was usually turned into my fault and that I was just not capable of handling the situation well.

When their grandmother finally moved to a small apartment that was 15 minutes away, the tension in the house relaxed a little bit. But she would often come to the bus stop for the school bus and she would make a point of coming to give small treat bags for the twins. Other kids on the bus were surprised and asked me why I never got anything. I was ashamed and just shrugged my shoulders, trying to hide in my seat and my stepsisters would answer: "because it is from our grandmother, she isn`t her granddaughter!"

It only got a bit better when I was in school and got my own room and could lock myself in. When I asked for attention or cried, I was called a "cry-baby". I was worried when my mother left, being alone with this family and she got upset with me for being so clingy. I asked her at some point why she treated the others almost better. Her reply was along the lines of needing to look like a good stepmother and that I had no reason to complain.

It Is Dark

It is dark, I am walking outside.
The stars are shining, but distant and cold.
There is not much light to show me the way.
Voices are coming from left and from right…
"This is wrong, no this is bad…"
I am now really scared.
I need some light, some warmth, some love.
I need some shelter from cool and from dark.

Where Is My Home?

I am walking alone, where is my home?
I think I had one once before, but I don`t
remember, it was so only decor.
Fine on the outside, neat and proper.
But on the inside, oh what a mess,
my mother cares less.
This shine has been working, a lie has been told.
Who wants to know the inside?
Is this how I get old?

Shadows

Shadows are chasing our hopes and dreams.
Where do this shadows come from?
They get up close and they try to destroy me.
But our dreams are much stronger and they
will prevail. We have the power and the
shadows will fail. This is the future, just keep
on dreaming. As this is the true way to dreams
of fulfillment.

My stepfather usually wasn`t around and when he couldn`t work overtime, he often go on bar trips, coming home drunk.

In the beginning my mother still picked him up, than she just ignored him, or sent us in to pick him up from the bar. I remember that he bought me a chocolate bar and told me to just wait a bit, asking me to sit in the corner. Let`s just say I am still very uncomfortable around drunk men. Healthy boundaries are gone and it gets inappropriate quickly…

From time to time I had to stay home from school and look after my mother when she wasn`t feeling well.

On one occasion I had to call the ambulance, as she thought she was having a heart attack. Thankfully it turned out to be a reaction to pitted fruit that caused colic. No doubt uncomfortable, but not a live threatening situation. But here I was trying to get my mother home without any money for a cab and my mother in her nightgown and housecoat, after worrying about her all night. Quite frankly it was easier going to school and daydreaming of being somewhere else, than being part of what was going on at home.

My maternal grandmother played an important role in my life and I spend every possible moment there, to avoid life in that so called home. She paid attention to me, showed me how to cook and did home work with me. I often slept in bed between my grandmother and

her second husband. He sure always criticized every-
thing she did and I think I seen her cry more than ever
really smile. The only time I ever seen her not sad, is
when we were in church. And it was very important for
her to go. Sometimes I wonder if this was because she
felt safer their? At least no one attacking her verbally,
resulted in her crying.

At some point I refused to stay any longer and
threatened to never come back, since he was so mean
to her. She cried even harder and bagged me to stay and
said she needed me, because she could not take this on
her own. I just could not bare to hurt her more, so I
got quiet and stayed. When I was about 13, she had a
stroke and stayed in the hospital for month. She was
suffering lots and her memory was getting really bad.
Crying to me, why I was not visiting more, since she
forgot we just had been there. She had hallucinations
after the brain was damaged from the stroke and later
on had to have one leg amputated, which left her dev-
astated. It was heartbreaking to see her getting worse
over the next six month. One day I came home from
school and my mother was on the phone talking about
her having died. I just looked at my mother, ran up-
stairs to my room, locked myself in as usual and cried
for hours on end. The only person ever to say that I
mattered and that actually wanted me. I was angry at
her for leaving me behind and wished I died as well. I
felt her presence for a long time after, or at least that is
what it felt like. And one day she was just really gone.

I guess I reached a point where I was ready to let go of her. But I was very interested and thought much about what comes after death. That interest never quite went away and it may be one of the reasons why I chose to work with older people in palliative care today.

My grandmother had a profound influence on me and I think she helped to lay the foundation of my believe in God that I have today. Aside from her daily marital struggles, she was very loving and caring and I am still very grateful for what she has given me!

Between my grandmother and a wonderful aunt, I think I turned out looking `normal` on the outside. They both made up a little for an otherwise terrifying life. My grandmother and my aunt showed me what a nurturing, loving woman looked and felt like. So don`t ever think your kind words are wasted. You may have a huge impact on a child, even if it seems like something so little to yourself. Just someone saying out loud how much they appreciate that child, can make a huge difference for that child.

Silent Screaming

*I walk as if in a dream, a dream I can not
wake up from. They call it life. I scream
for help, want to get out.
Nobody seems to hear me, yet the louder
I scream, the further they seem to run.*

So the lesson is: scream silent!

*This dream called life, seems like it will kill
my soul. Yet I have to keep smiling,
nobody wants to know.
Reality is, everyone is busy with themselves…*

*I scream for help, want to get out.
Nobody seems to hear me, yet the louder I scream,
the further they seem to run.*

*Again the lesson is: scream silent!
Nobody wants to know…*

Lonely

This feeling they call being lonely…
It can catch you and it carries you away.
Away from feeling loved. Away from feeling
a part of. Away from sanity.
This feeling they call lonely…
It gives you this mask.

It helps you to hide the true self.
It stops you from living your life.
This feeling of being lonely, it wraps you
in like a blanket. You feel like you can`t
get out.

No matter how much you try, now matter
how many people are around you, you still
feel so alone.

Controlling

You think you are so strong,
but really you are weak.
So scared of your own weakness,
you want me to believe you have
control over me.
By hurting me you can look away
from your own pain.
How small and little do you really feel?
Is that than cruel or real?
You ignore and embarrass,
make me feel ashamed.
It is never you that is to blame.
It is time you looked at your own pain.
Quit being controlling, as this game is
your shame!

My stepbrother really struggled with losing his mother, an absent father, new stepmother and his grandmother filling him with resentment and lies.

He either pretty much ignored me, or made fun of me. So when he suddenly acted different and paid attention to me, I thought he changed his mind.

He started with allowing me into his room, which was usually a big no. And I did not notice that he asked any of his actual sisters to hang out in his room as well. So I felt special and was hoping I would finally be accepted. Than the memory gets incomplete and I don`t know exactly how he convinced me to get on his bed…

I felt sick though, having him on-top of me and "practicing" on me, as he called it.

And for the longest time I blocked the whole memory out, as it made me feel even more worthless and dirty. I always had the memory of when he was being nice and asked me into his room and I remember playing with his green sliding ruler, but the rest was blocked. Until my son was at about the same age, that I was when this happened.

I was raised to be a "good" girl and this… Well, for the longest time I thought it was my fault for not fighting back. But no one would have believed me anyway. And I truly thought I deserved this. After all, wouldn`t my mother have protected me if this was wrong to happen?

The Thing about NO

*NO, is a word used more often
than you think. The sales person
does not like it. The tax department
does not accept it.*

*Every day there is someone using it
and someone that does not like it.
But the NO`s that really hurt,
are the once that don`t get heard.*

*There is a tiny voice, sometime just
a bagging in the eyes.
There is a person bagging NO.
And the other doesn`t want to know.*

*These unheard NO`s will turn a life
into a nightmare. And if I tell you
now how much it hurts and you
don`t want to know, then maybe in
your mind, you will have a silent NO!*

Broken Trust

It hurts so deep, you wouldn`t know.
After all you rather see the show.
The inside is broken. Broken by words,
hands and minds of the past.
I don`t know how long this will last?

I gave You my hand, I gave You my heart.
Oh why is this so awful and hard.
I truly believed and I thought I was safe.
But You abandoned me when I needed
You the most.

Where do I go now and what should I do?
For I am so scared to turn again towards You.
My laughter is silent and my heart beats, but quiet.
Don`t see any future, don`t see any hope.
They say it`s god`s will, so I take it and stay broke.

Growing Up

This is what I remember of growing up. Most days it was quite hard. Abandoned by parents, locked in a room. My feelings daily terrorized and denied.
When will you start to open your eyes?
The dignity was taken away, made fun of and threatened by you and the rest.
Where was the loving? Was this your best?

When I look back the things I remember for almost every day in that old calendar, was mocking, critizise and you yelled. It was so rare that you have just held. When I took the courage and told you I was hurting, you turned around and played it down.
Drowned out my feelings of needing some love.
Even though this now might sound harsh. To twist and turn the truth, even deny some of it. But really, don`t you think this shoe does fit?
There was also good, I won`t deny that, but how much bad had I to take for that… You still don`t know and you may never, but facing the truth won`t go away forever.

Motherless

Sometimes I feel like a motherless child,
wandering and walking a long way from home.
The road is winding and sometimes dark.
Why does this all feel so lonely and hard?

A little girl, so lost on her way,
crying and calling for someone to hear her.
She keeps on walking along this path
and hopes one day there will be a place she loves.

A place to rest, feel loved and call home.
Somewhere she really is not alone…

When I was around 14, I got more curious about where I came from. I was fortunate to have contact to my older cousin in Pakistan through letters. I had found out from her that my father had re-married and that this relationship resulted in two girls and a boy. Wow, two half-sisters and a half-brother. It felt like having family after all. Although no one actually knew where he was living, last she heard, he was in England. He met his new wife there, but since she was of German decent like my mother, anything was possible.

I was so happy and excited about having half-sisters and a half-brother, finally someone who had something in common with me. I thanked God for this positive news.

Than one night I had a dream. It seemed like my dad was visiting my grandparents with my cousin. Usually my step-grandpa did not like "foreigners", but in that dream he complimented my cousin's gorgeous, black, very long, open hair. I noticed a white car just past the hedge, parked along the roadside. The license plate started with BI (Germany has initials for the city the car is registered in, on the license plate). Thinking about this rather strange dream, one day I decided I had nothing to lose. So I called information and got all the numbers that were listed under my dad's last name for that city. One name was a woman's name, but somehow stood out?! I started to call that number and then got scared. I started again and a man with an accent answered. I hung up the phone again, unsure

WORDS FOR THE UNSPEAKABLE

of what to say. What was I thinking? This was a man who obviously did not want me. And what was I to say? Then I remembered that I did not want him back in my life and my mother did not agree either. But I sure wanted the opportunity to meet my brother and sisters. So I took a deep breath and tried again and when he picked up the phone and connected again, I explained who I was looking for and it turned out to be my father. It got silent for a moment and then I heard him sobbing on the other end. He just kept saying: "I am sorry dear, I am so sorry…".

To make a long story short, he wanted to see me. I reluctantly agreed to meet him in the city I was closest to and going to school at. (I grew up on the country). I sort of had a relationship with my father again, but still untrusting and distant. I did get to meet my half-sisters and half-brother, which I am still grateful for today. Their mom was a bit unsure and afraid I guess?! But I instantly connected to my sisters and brother and I felt I now belonged somewhere, at least on some level.

Now becoming a teenager, so many things change and I was no exception to that. Even though being in an all girl school, boys started to notice me and showed interest. I was generally to shy and unsure of how to react. And although curious, much too scared to trust any of them. I had a relationship with a six year older boy, or actually young man. I was confused that my step-dad seemed to approve of him, when otherwise he would not approve of the idea of a boyfriend. One night, after dating for half a year, he wanted more and I refused to go past where I was really not comfortable. I never heard of him again after that. No good bye, or explanation. I felt hurt and it took me a long time trying to understand and somehow figure out what I had done wrong.

When I met my future husband a few months later, I was not interested in a relationship of any kind. He was persistent and told me it was ok to be just friends and kept showing up every day. We ended up talking lots, in person, over the phone and most of the time over CB radio. The pain we shared, of losing a father early on and having to live with alcoholism in the family, made it easy to connect and we starting to trust each other. My father however reminded me of what a proper girl behaved like and at the same time wanted to know if I was serious with this young man. Then proceeded to tell me that the reason he asked me was, that I was promised to my cousin in Pakistan, who was two years old than me, 18. He was a college student. All I had to do was fly over, marry him and then could come back. He pulled out a picture, as if to convince me he was a good looking young man. Had I been in Pakistan, this likely would have ended up different. I just told my father that I was not raised to be an obedient Pakistani women and I could not agree to an arranged marriage. I did start to feel bad about the "un-proper" relationship I was having with my boyfriend though. But deep down I thought of myself as damaged and unworthy anyway. My father thankfully never found out…

He eventually accepted my husband later on, after realizing we were committed to each other. My only regret was, that he never made it to our wedding. And I never really quite knew how to feel about him or relate to him. He came to the hospital when my son was born and was a proud grandfather though.

Unfortunately, when our son was still small, my father ended up quite sick. I was told not to bather to come by his wife, since he was in an artificial coma. I eventually decided to go and visit anyway, realizing I would not get to say to him what I needed to get out. Then came the news that he had passed away. I did not just grieved that loss of a father, but also that I still never really knew what a father really was. We drove for a couple of hours in hopes I would get at least to pay my last respects and get some kind of closure. But when we got there, the imam was there and then the coffin was sealed for the flight to Pakistan. We did not have the money as a young couple and family, for me to fly and attend the funeral, let alone for both of us. And somehow the idea to fly by myself into this country without a male escort, seemed somewhat unsafe as well.

So here I was on my own again. No real closure and important things left unsaid.

He Went Away Twice

When I was little you were there.
Showed sometimes that you would care.
Then suddenly you made me cry and
found amusement in my pain.
You left and didn`t say good bye.

You hardly cared that I was crying
and on the inside slowly dying.
You had someone that you cared more for.
I was alone and thought I was bad.
What had I done to loose your love?
It truly killed a part of me.
The trust was broken, a bond was cut.
I truly needed your arms and love.

Now I`ve grown up and am alive,
but can`t stop thinking I was not good enough.
And even though I have known love, will hurt,
when you, I am thinking of.

Future

I am sitting and writing, hoping and dreaming.
My mind goes astray, or is that okay?
These feelings they tell the directions to go.
But where will they take me?
What if they betray me?
The future is uncertain. When will we be
pulling the curtain?
I wonder what life is trying to teach me?

But I have to trust what lies ahead.
I only pray it won`t be to bad…
Oh please, let`s join hands and let`s all
say a prayer. If we are all willing, we can
make it better!

Love & Protection...

Does not loving mean protecting?
A dog is loyal, he would protect me,
because he loves me.

The animals instinctively come
up with ways to safe their young.
They sometimes even give their
life to protect them from a predator.

So here I`m asking you again...
Does not loving mean protecting?

Pain

Abandoned by parents, hurt in the
process. Abused in the past.
Even you God choose not to listen.
And now broken and tired there is
yet more I am to carry.

The inside is empty, it just feels numb.
For if I feel, the pain would kill.
Emotions go crazy, the mind is adrift.
A hand and a smile really is a big gift.

The trust in oneself is gone and hurt.
Love is replaced with anger and pain.
The happiness is gone and the future
looks hopeless. As it seems the pain
does not want to leave you.
It gets in the way and cuts you off.
Takes you away from those you truly love.
It makes you a slave and it puts you in chains.

Back to being a teenager, the emotional and other changes of a teenager are hard enough, but adding in feelings of abandonment, verbal and sexual abuse, makes it tough to see hope and find the desire to stay alive. I hit a low point when everything that was looking hopeful fell apart and I was back in a deep depression. There was so much emotional pain that I just could not stand it anymore. I took a raiser from the bathroom, went to bed crying, put music on and cut my wrist.

Somehow my mother wanted something and came to my room, which generally never happened. I guess God decided it was not my time to go yet and my mother finding me like that, she put a pressure bandage on and told me 'I was a silly girl'. And that I had no right, or reason to do this! It was never talked about again after, as if it did not happen. But I know it did, since I still have the scar today that sometimes reminds me of how lost and unworthy I felt that day.

Did You Know Me?

You run so fast from yourself that you forget to stop and see me. I have stopped and hit a wall and really can`t go on no more. I have no strength left and am giving up.

But what is your comment to that? That I am only a dumb girl and really have no right to end this cold and lonely life. Who gave you the right to judge my feelings as cold as ice? What is there that makes you scared?

So while I`m down and am there bleeding, you add salt to injury. And than your answer to all this, that something wrong with my head there is.

I`m telling you it is my heart. It is running over with pain and loss of trust.

Like Drowning

You feel like struggling, like fighting for air.
Big waves keep coming, crushing right over your head.
You kick and you fight, swim up with all might.
It makes you feel cold and you get so exhausted.
At some point you wonder, is this going to end?
The water is deep, is cold and is frightening.
The body is hurting, like it was hit by lightening.
You think just give up and slowly sink lower.
But then somehow you worry for loved ones.
How would they feel if you would not make it?
That gives back some strength in your arms and
your legs.
And so you continue to struggle for air.
You get a moment with your head out of water,
enough to make it while you go back under.

You Know Who You Are...

You probably don`t know the pain you have caused. The shame, the frustration and the pain will always stay here.

Some days it feels fine, than others are hardly benign. It robs the laughter, just is one painful disaster. It feels like it strips one of it`s humanity. Shakes to the core and makes you think you deserve it. The heart is bleeding, the soul gets out of control. I hope you got what you wanted. If not, it is such a shame and only you are for all this to blame.

Some days I hate you, others I don`t. But hopefully one day all this will be over. And just maybe we all are not just older. This pain I will carry for the rest of my life. And I only hope you will hurt no one else. Please stop and think, as your own soul will carry this burden until the end.

The Unspoken Message

"Go to your room, I don`t want to see you..."
What does that mean?
Are you really not mean?

A `time out` would be different.
It would not imply that you are sick of me.
It would not have meant that you have stopped
loving me.

What were your intentions?
Did you even know?
So much was taken, if you'd only known.

The words so unkind, the message was hurtful.
And now I have to learn to get past them...

Memories

Don`t you think of memories as something pleasant?
Like a forever lasting present?

The photo album collects all these.
From festivals and special trips
a memory to have is it.
But have you also yet considered that sometimes
the past is better when forgotten?

For some of us the memories are painful once.
You will not find these in an album, but deep
inside of someone`s mind.

These are not collected treasures, but memories
that haunt your dreams!

4

The Search for Answers

Somehow I guess I tried to escape the feeling of not being good enough and being "damaged goods" by asking to let me go to a catholic all girl school in the city, an hour drive on the bus. I just did not want to have to deal with boys. I believe in some ways that was actually good for me. I just did not understand what was truly behind those feelings. After making it through the isolation of the language and cultural barrier, the loss of a father, verbal, emotional and sexual abuse, I did not expect much out of life.

What took me the longest was to accept that my mother stays in denial, to protect herself. I kept trying, wishing and hoping for a so called normal mother-daughter relationship. I continued to go over and over the need for a loving, nurturing mother. I believed what I was told and taught growing up and even continued some of those messages in negative self-talk…

"If I am only trying harder and do enough, she will love me, right?"

I remember when she got angry, after calling me to come back from the field, I was sitting under a tree playing with the dog. I must have not heard her calling the first time, but she was convinced I did not listen on purpose. When I did come to the house, she was waiting with the wooden cooking spoon. I got hit with it before I knew what was happening. I remember rolling on the ground, balled up like a baby and covering my face. Crying, I repeated to ask her to stop. She kept hitting me randomly wherever she could hit. At some point I just gave up and stayed quiet and then the spoon broke in half and she stopped.

She told me to go to my room without supper. Quite frankly, I was glad to get away from her and I was too sore to worry about food anyway.

Looking back at that now, it is not clear to me why the not hearing her would cause that kind of a reaction?! It might have left her feeling out of control and triggered her anger and I was there to take it out on.

Return to Pain

*The mask comes of for a short time. It has protected me
for years, covers up all my deepest fears. Someone has
lifted it oh just a bit, it left me panicking and sick. What
will I do if someone sees how awful all my inside is?*

*It is pain and anger, cooked and old, that really still has
a good hold. What can I do and live a life, so no one
knows how deep`s this ice.*

*You forced me to stop and look. It hurts and scares me,
takes my breath. What do I do with so much mess? So I
turned to God and scream and yell, say NO again to all
this pain. But even that is all in vain.*

*What is there for me to learn, but that live gets you back
at every turn. They say time heals, but really it appears
that it just preserves it well.*

*Who has the answer? Cause I sure don`t. And am left to
wonder, is this how I get old?*

But coming through those experiences also made me the person that I am. And I did believe in Christ already, which was probably something that gave me strength on some level.

So life continued and I met my future husband at 16, as mentioned earlier. He survived a very abusive father and watched some horrific stuff growing up. One of them was to see his dad slowly dying of cancer. He never learned how to properly treat a woman, but he did care and choose to learn to do things better over the years. Determined not to repeat his father's abusive behavior. He never drank and helped himself by agreeing to participate in an anger management course and later on counseling. We both made huge mistake over the years, but our friendship always helped to keep working on the relationship and marriage.

Six month after first dating, we were engaged. And once I turned 18 I moved out on my own. My stepfather laughed at me and told me I would be crawling back after 3 weeks. Well, whatever it took, I was determined not to go back there! I don't really know anymore how I managed, but I was sitting in a dark, cold apartment and barely had enough money to eat. But I was out, safer! And being independent in my own apartment, I finally had time to find myself.

I never wanted to get married, after having seen only negative examples of what a husband is, growing up. But the relationship with my partner (now my husband) got more serious and he eventually also moved in. Which at least made the financial situation a little bit better.

Thoughts

My thoughts they are drifting,
like leaves in a wild storm.
They are hard to control,
they are all over like a swarm.
But I do have to try, as hard as it may be.
How hard is it to find peace and forgiveness for me?
I know that the waves of anger,
loneliness and frustration will settle.
Than I will know I have won this battle.
To quieter shores this journey will take me.
But I will have learned so much in the process.
Through all this, the good and the bad,
my friend you have been there and may
god bless you for all you have shared!

Magic Moments

When you start to face things and open up,
there just could be understanding and love.
A little gesture, a smile and a touch,
are giving the other person so much.

A flower is just a pretty thing,
but combined with sincere words of caring,
they become so much more.
You should find the strength and go explore.

When the moment comes and you trust yourself,
facing the pain and lies of the past,
it opens a door like magic to go and come back
from your past.
All the things you have faced that were tragic,
become less powerful and allow a breath of
fresh air and some light, where before it was dark.

For a moment in time you can tell who you are.
Be honest and face some of the truth,
that you have hidden away for so many years.

To a person that does not judge and believes,
show all that you are, the pain and the love.
As being a whole person inside and out,
is what one hopes to achieve when speaking out loud.

The Power of the Word

*Words are strong when they belong. A word like love can
mean the world, when said in honesty.*

*Than on the other hand a painful, hurtful one, you will
never know what kind of damage it has done.*

*A slap, a hit stays outside on the skin. As much as that
will hurt, it can heal when given time. The hateful,
angry word will go deep into once core. And when you
really go explore, you`ll find those are the dangerous once.
They`ll take your trust and break your heart.*

*And even though you`ve given time, they leave you
powerless and numb…*

Than at age 20 we got married, one year earlier than we had planned. Later that year our son was born. We were proud and scared at the same time, like most new parents. Only there was more, I just was not quite sure yet what.

In 1997 we moved to Canada. Something I had been longing for, as far as I can remember. Only after meeting my husband so young, I did not think this would actually happen.

With having to start over, struggling to make enough money, having left our friends behind and trying to be a "good wife" and a mother to our son, I felt pushed to a breaking point, when old memories from the sexual abuse started to surface in my conscious again. In 1999 I could not cope any longer and just did not know how to deal with, what is called flashbacks. What saved me than was the Sexual Assault Center. I went to the hospital on my own, because of my suicidal feelings again. But traditional psychiatry does not really understand the actual issues and a "chemical" treatment does not solve anything. It can help cope for a short while, but only a trained professional that knows how to deal with trauma, will be of lasting improvement.

The antidepressants left me feeling nothing. I wasn`t crying all the time anymore, but I could not feel joy or happiness either and now felt really messed up. I figured I had not much to lose and started with an intake appointment at the Sexual Assault Center where

I met Shirley for the first time. I was scared having to talk about what was going on and felt so ashamed of myself. How could I ever tell anybody what was coming up in my dreams, asleep or daytime now…I could not imagine anyone would understand, nor did I wanted anyone to know this "dirty little secret". And I was still much too shy to talk about such things anyway.

I am still thankful to god for sending Shirley into my life as my councilor. She was very gentle and made every step very safe, letting me decide how fast I was able to go with this. And when she told me I did not have to talk about the actual rape, I could just work on the feelings, I was so relieved. For the first time in my life I felt like someone seemed to see the true me and understood what I was struggling with. Now things started to make sense. And I started with individual counseling and then joined group therapy with other women facing similar experiences.

I was at last not so alone with this anymore. I learned about what abuse is and how it affects people. I started to see that a lot of the reactions are not from being crazy, but are a reaction to an unsafe environment. That abuse can change how the brain works and can cause post-traumatic stress and often can cause chronic diseases, especially hormonal, like e.g. diabetes, insomnia, eating disorders, all types of addictions and much more than what most people are aware of.

This healing journey is an ongoing process, but being able to talk to people that understand how one feels and reacts, is a big support system. I believe we can help each other. While each individual has to do his, or her work, we give each other strength and the support we did not have in the past, when the abuse was going on. But I know for myself and probably many others, without divine intervention and guidance, this would still be a hopeless, vicious cycle. Since I turned back to God, I see more hope and have more strength to overcome hurtful, damaging feelings, which before kept me trapped for month at a time in a deep depression. My good times are getting longer and I find joy in my life now, which I rarely had as a child. I still have hurtful memories and feelings come up from time to time. And especially nights seem to be hard to manage at times. I keep waking up, or resent going to sleep, not being able to control what I dream about. And early part of the night were always an unsafe time in bed. Towards morning my step dad and the rest of the family would finally be in bed and not a threat anymore. So even today, I tend to sleep much better in the morning hours.

Which brings up a memory, of where my stepfather was drunk again. And this time not just happy and tired as usual. After much yelling and physical struggling, my mother finally was able to look him in the bedroom. Only as drunk as he was, he came through the balcony that joined my parent`s bedroom and my room window. My window was on tilt, as it was a warm summer night and with some kind of a tool, he tried to open it more, so he could get in. I pretended to sleep and pulled the blanket over my head. I tried to make no sound and held my breath as long as I could, tears running down my face, praying he would not succeed to get in.

It seemed like hours and I don`t remember how this ended… nor do I want to know!

Truth Is Cold and Deep

*Here I am drifting in the past. The feelings are strong
and vast. I feel some love and a lot of hurt. They say time
heals wounds and pain, but really it does not.*

*The only way to get beyond is facing all this hurt and
feel it till your lost in it. It takes so much strength and
courage. Not everyone can make it through and drowns
in all of these emotions. Yet honest life and happiness can
not be found without the cold sea of distrust and pain.
You have to swim and feel them all to get beyond to
happy shores.*

*I only hope I have the strength to keep on going, as I
know that someone waits with open arms at those heeling
shores. He has to swim as much as I and knows how cold
and deep it gets. So let`s just hope there is some light, that
keep alive in us the fight.*

Washed Away

Feelings they come and go, don`t leave you in control over when and where. They wash over you like a wave. Take you with it and make you drift.

These feelings they flood your heart with hurt or with love. They are in control and they take you on a journey. You better sit back and hang on for the ride.

Those feelings are strong, but they let you know you are alive…

I Had Enough

*If I don`t feel it I can not write it. There is not a chance
I can make up and lie about it.*

*You said with my head there was something wrong.
You lied about that, I know it`s not true, as I know have
professional proof.*

*This only shows how silly you are. Just labeling
convenient, instead of confess. Somewhere deep inside
yourself lies a mess.*

*So I tell you now, you work on yourself and stop to abuse
me. As otherwise I have no choice, but to avoid you
completely.*

*If I don`t feel it, I can not write it. There is no chance I
can make it up and lie about it.*

A lot of that life seems like a blur today and I keep telling myself it is over and in the past now. Often I refer to it as my old life.

I am certainly a happier person and have hobbies I enjoy. Especially my animals were very important at that time already and they are still today. When no one else is there to talk to you or enjoy your company, animals like a rabbit, my cat and my horse were always happy to see me. These four legged creatures always let you know where you stand. Either they don`t like you and they do not go about that behind your back, or they do love you. Even if you are having a bad day, are grumpy, wear makeup or not. They sure can teach us the correct meaning of unconditional love! They have such a wonderful way of healing a broken heart. I feel blessed by God for sending me special "little helpers". I have seen in my own life and others, what a therapeutic effect they can have. And they sure can make one laugh. And who has not felt better after a good laugh?

Other things that have a big effect on the mood is music. It can be stimulating, exciting, relaxing, bring us closer to God, but also can make a person more angry. So careful what kind of music you are choosing. You may not realize that it actually makes you do things you had no intentions of before. But wisely chosen, can be wonderful to put an anxious mind at ease. It is good, there is a wide variety of music, so everyone can find something that fit's the personality and mood. It is no wonder that the great composers were so involved when writing their best pieces of music. It has a way of transforming emotions.

Another thing that has often helped me is simply going for a walk. Seeing trees, flowers, running water or the stars. And even better yet when you feel the wind in your face or a warm rain drop. It somehow let`s you remember to be in the moment. And while you are in the moment, you can not be stuck in the past at the same time. It is a form of grounding and in most cases it is very helpful. Personally that is why I like being out there between our animals, just feeling the grass or their fur and feel safe in the present. The past will catch up at some point again, especially when not active and the mind can go racing, like when driving and sleeping. But surrounded with my animals, I can stay safe a little longer.

Feeling the loss of safety is a major consequence when living with an abusive past. If people you would expect to be concerned for you, like parents, family members and life partners and they are not, then why should a stranger be respectful and concerned? So you expect the worst out of everyone around you and trusting is something that becomes extremely difficult. Once you lose the trust in yourself, the way to recovery becomes hopeless. I am not sure if I can explain this well to someone who has not lived through those feelings. But an experience I have had, might explain what the result may look like.

I prefer to not get into the why, as that is not important here and I even wondered if I should include this in the book. But it needs to get told, so people are made aware of how bad the situations in women shelters can be, mostly because of a lack of funding.

This is not to complain about my husband, or play on people's sympathy. But without getting into too much detail, there were a few major mistakes made by people close to me and it ended up in a heartbreaking crisis, that almost cost us our marriage and the closeness to a family member I had treasured before I was betrayed by her.

Let's just say I needed to get out of the way and fast. I did not have a lot of friends I felt I could turn to. And at moments like that, thinking is not really something you can rely on. You actually just react. My son still too young to be left alone and I did not think he would have been safe being left behind anyway. Being desperate and out of options, I called my mother and told her that I needed to leave our son with her for a bit. There was no shelter space with children left.

I felt bad enough and now also guilty for rushing things and leaving my son behind at my mothers. But at least he was in familiar surrounding and with people he knew. Than with just a handful of things I had packed in a hurry to make it for a couple of days, I drove back and found the inner city shelter for women. I felt a big lump in my throat when going up the elevator and was checked by the door, to ensure safety for everyone inside. The feeling of betrayal, anger and fear kept growing inside of me.

Once inside a support worker told me to just have a seat and someone would see me as soon as possible. And in a site remark advised me to hang on to my belongings at all times, since there was a high rate of thefts. She was worried that it be hard to find something to eat, as they were so much over capacity and had been laid out for 70, but had now about 100 women. But I ensured her it was ok and that I was not hungry anyway. Getting a chair was even harder and once I had a place in the corner I just looked around me and noticed so many sad looking women around me. There facial expression looked empty and hopeless and often angry. One native lady, very young looking and she would have been so pretty, would it not have been for the fresh knife scares across her left cheek. A thin, blond women that looked full of anger and resentment, talked to me about one day getting out of this. As if she was talking about prison. Than another woman by the window with long dark hair stared out of the window, her eyes were beautiful, but empty. She did not seem to notice anything around her. Someone finally came and talked to me about my situation and offered me a make shift mattress in the laundry room as all the beds were full. She hoped that something would open up in the next couple of days, but it was somewhat unpredictable and she could not promise a bed. So I tried to settle down and tried to reflect on what had happened. How did I end up in this mess? I felt terribly alone, but after all a feeling I was used to already.

I tried to call home, but that just left me even more discouraged and I tried to find a private corner to cry in. Not that there really was one. Women around me tried on some level to be nice, but most were so absorbed in their own pain, that there was little comfort. The very air seemed filled with pain, negative charged air and the strongest feeling of hopelessness I had felt so far. If there is an emotional hell, this is what it must be like!

I tried to distract myself by watching television and the local news was on. People were talking about their problem with the trouble-shooter and all I could think about was, that most people did not even know what real trouble actually felt like. My situation kept sneaking up in my mind and there was no running from the pain. How could I have been so blind and trusted again. I felt so broken into pieces on the inside that I was sure there was no way to heal this. I could not understand why again the closest people were the once that hurt me so deeply. Was there no one left to care?

Then I seen the girl with the long hair and empty eyes dressed up and going out with just a thin coat over, well not much of clothes at all. Kind of a risky way to dress I was thinking and sure not something I would ever be brave enough to try. Then I watched from the window looking down how she stood by the corner and only a little while later it hit me. She mate comments earlier about nothing would matter anymore anyway and seeing her getting into a car, I know felt heartbroken for her. I realized she was selling her body, as she figured it was damaged and unwanted anyway and there was not much left of dignity and self-worth. So she had completely given up and it explained why her eyes looked like they did, just starred right though me and looked so empty. I wonder how many women ended up in this trade, because of abusive pasts with no one here to show them that they care? I could not control the flow of my tears now and I felt like rolling up into a ball and just stop to exist. I tried to lay down on the make shift mat on the floor in a corner in the laundry room between a washer and a dryer. Of course there was no real privacy, as women were just everywhere. So I was lying down facing the wall and continued to sob as quietly as a I could. But just a short while after it got loud and there were two women arguing loudly. Obscenities were exchanged and it quickly became very scary. I tried to be very quiet and just curled closer around my belongings, pulling the thin blanket just a little higher. I hoped they would not notice me and just pretended to be sleeping. I was just not in a frame of mind to be able to handle this. The situation quickly escalated and one woman drew a small pocket knife.

Some women yelled for help and they tried to keep the women physically apart. It looked like a scene from a movie, from a prison fight scene, only this was real and I was in it. They had called the police and they showed up very fast. The only men ever allowed in there.

They started to take statements and one of the officers looked at me as if to say: What brought a women like you in here tonight?

I told them what I had seen and then decided I could not stand this any longer. Anything was better than this! So I left and stayed in my car. It was cold and my mind was racing on what to do. I must have driven around and a few times, I was thinking of just taking too many pills and than just hit a tree. But again something was there to protect me and I ended up at home in the morning. My husband was about to leave for work and instead of yelling at me, he looked shocked seeing me in the state I was. I was cowered in between the couches of our living room and just bagged him to leave and not touch me, crying still uncontrollably. I think he really did not know how to handle this and thankfully left and went to work. After some time I was able to settle down a bit and I remember feeling so exhausted. I locked all the doors, closed the blinds and crawled finally into my own bed.

If there is anything to be learned from my experience, there needs to be better solutions for women trapped in violent situations. It is just this lack of help that sends the message that we as a society just don`t care and that they do not deserve to be safe, unless they can contribute to society. Well, if we showed we care and that they matter to us, than just maybe they can find the hope and strength needed to become a healthy, stable person that can be a viable part of society…

So Deep

How deep is the ocean, how far are the stars?
It would not have room for all the pain that
gets suffered for someone else`s gain.

Who makes it stop? This may come as a shock.
But really don`t you think it is all in vain?
I can no longer carry all this pain...

As deep as the ocean, as far and wide,
my heart turns cold, as cold as ice.
The beating stops, the body feels numb.
Am scared to breath and take more pain.
It goes so deep into every vein.
It feels so hopeless, cold and dark.
Would there be room on Noah`s ark?
I rest now and take my leave
and may it only be so brief.

I let that cloud take me away,
so maybe I will forget about yesterday.

True Friends

"It`s just a dog" is what you said.
They bark, they poop, they shed.
All I can think of, have you looked in the mirror yet?

They may a nuisance be to you.
To me they are a special gift.
A friend that`s there and asks no questions.

They trust your word and love your touch.
Giving you love is never to much.

They comfort me when I am sad.
They calm me down when I am mad.
They help protect me when I`m scared.
They make me laugh and love me back.

Do you really have a friend like that?

In Love with Music

Everyone talks about it,
but did you feel it?
This feeling that lets you think
you are dreaming, floating away
on a cloud of emotions.
Everyone dreams of finding it,
wishing that one day to find the words for it.

Today I`m in love with music.
It can make you laugh and can make you
cry at the same time. It is real and a dream
at the same time. It can give you
goose bumps and can make you feel warm.
All over at once… It carries your dream
with the flow of the wind. Music can help
tell the world that you care. Sharing, expressing
and so much more. Music, a wonderful way to
share your love…

Having written down how I felt through the last couple of years, it is interesting to see how things have changed. And there really is a moving forward and even more, an understanding of past events. The pain of the past never really went away, but it also is not as threatening anymore, once healing occurs. It is not forgetting what happened, as that does not work anyway, but rather an understanding of the events and finding ways to accept it and then letting go of it. Accepting the pain and the loss of an innocent childhood, of feeling loved and protected. I can start to allow myself to feel the pain, go through the process of grieving those losses and than just be ok with being that person. Letting go of people that are not supportive and accepting of who we really are.

Remember that we are perfect in god's image and that he cares and loves us, broken and not perfect. The biggest challenge that we all face is, to accept and love ourselves!

I sure am struggling with accepting myself for who I really am. But being a sexual abuse victim is not something I chose or asked for. It is not what defines me, or decides if I can be happy or not. I know that there are people right now struggling with a much worse fate and others that never knew so far, what trauma is.

But it is us, oneself that has a choice to make. I can give in to the pain and let bad things take over and win. Or I can decide to not live in the pain anymore, look for positive things, surround myself with positive people and pray for healing and peace in my heart.

I believe by deciding to be a survivor, rather than stay the victim, we can make a big step in our healing journey. Of course there will be set backs and on some days it feels like a viscous circle that never ends. But the spiral moves out and we do eventually heal, one piece, one layer and one memory at a time. I like to think of my past as the part of the caterpillar, the present as being in the cocoon and the future as the life of a butterfly. At first ugly, unattractive and fat. Than big changes, hard work and lots of sleep. But in the end, life is light, colorful and beautiful.

Almost Like a Butterfly

This almost feels like a way to become
a butterfly. I start out so ugly, slow and fat,
as one would look upon a caterpillar.
Than something tells you here is
something wrong and you have
bigger things to learn.

You go through a long and difficult time.
Withdraw from the world and stay on
you own. For how long, I am not sure?
I only hope that by the end, out comes
a new me, something beautiful and light.

Free to just take off and go wherever you please.
Make people smile and float in a breeze.
I hope that one day too, I will come out
of this cocoon, as light and new.
Almost as colorful and bright as a butterfly`s
first flight.
The life renewed…!

Survivor

This is so hard, I know I am trying to get better.
But this feelings are strong. Making me feel
like I don`t belong.
I am a survivor, does that mean I am a fighter?
When will I be able to control my feelings?
Or will they always have control over me?
This is frightening and I am getting tired.
But I know I want my life back, be in control
and find my peace.
Not just for myself, but for others as well.

Not Sure

*Not sure where I am now? The anger comes and goes,
takes the control, than gives it back. I`ve got a few
answers, or so I believe. Just scared that I made them up,
as I need something to cling to and believe.*

*God says he heard me and did not just leave me. But
rather send me my friend and gave him the strength. If
this is true it would mean a lot. But how do I know I
didn`t just make it up?*

*This is the problem with so much abuse. You lose the
trust in your feelings and thoughts. How can I get to be
assertive enough and trust myself?*

*I need to find some strength within. But without
guidance it is hard to do. Does this feel sometimes the
same to you?
I need to keep fighting and have to find a way. I just
wish this would not be so confusing and I could trust
myself, till I get back on my way.
This journey which we call life, sometimes it`s lonely,
sometimes it feels alive.*

5

Life as a Survivor

In 2007 I was getting to the point where I had a fairly good idea of why I am struggling so much in my life and understood more how past traumatic events effect me today. But I did not want all these unpleasant feelings anymore. I wanted so much to feel normal and free of pain. All this stuffed down anger over years started to come up and made it hard to function some days. It is like a bottle that is under pressure, when you start open it a little after shaking it, there is so much build up pressure, it is hard to let off just a bit of steam. But it needed to be released, so I could move on.

I went back trying to analyze the past again, somehow trying to make sense out of it. Then I figured if I just get the responsible person held accountable in court, I would have justice and be better off. I discussed with my mother if I should get my step-brother charged or not. I wasn't even sure if that would work in Germany the same way as here. The justice system is quite different. Here in Canada, sexual assault has no statute of limitations. So by just having my memory more complete now, I could have had charges laid, even after so many years.

Well I should have known better than to discuss any of this with my mother. She got all defensive right away and was worried how this would look like for the family. And told me I should consider how this might affect his children he has out of different relationships. There was no concern over how I was dealing with that experience. She was clearly trying to protect a person who chooses not to have contact with her. He made clear that he does not consider us to be family, when after my step-father`s death the house and farm land was split up and whoever wanted the property, needed to pay out the rest. We did not feel right to leave my mother all alone and so offered to pay them out and renovate the upstairs for my husband, son and myself. At first everyone was happy with that solution and we had the mortgage approved. Than all of a sudden my step-brother was against it, being that I was not part of the family. The house and property was sold to a neighbor, who bulldozed the house down. My mother moved with us to northern Germany, where we had found a house and my mother moved in there with us. There was no more contact to my step-brother after that.

So after all this, she was still protecting him? I felt rejected and hurt all over again. And I do not even believe now I would want a court trial anymore. It does not make anything go away, or changes the past. I would get so much more from a letter saying: "I have hurt you and I am sorry".

I actually have forgiven already what needed to be forgiven for my own sake. I would have been trapped at that point, if I would have not been able to move on. So called justice, would have made no difference, it is probably more an illusion. Somehow I was now more hurt by my mother's point of few. After living in another country, being not in that family anymore and being in a safe place now. She still chose to be in denial of the past and "plays it safe", instead of supporting me. I felt abandoned by her all over again! And all those old bottled up feelings were suddenly all back. It was no longer an old painful history, but something real and happening right now. It was something new, but tied into old not healed wounds. And I started to realize the loss of having a loving mother all over again. I just tried to distant myself and somehow just cope. With her getting quite demanding and complaining that I would not call her, I felt pretty stressed out.

She was still expecting that I would make time for her concerns, but generally would cut me off when I started to talk about my problems.

Than eventually I had enough courage to confront

my mother about how I really felt. I told her in writing how I saw the past and growing up. It did not leave any room for interpretation and was even harsh in telling her she gave up the right to call herself my mother, when she abandoned me emotionally like that. I had to send this before I lost my courage and I did broke down after that. Waiting for the big punishment to follow! My husband had to drive me to the emergency room the next day, finding me on the kitchen floor, crying heavily, completely unable to function. I had watched how the horses came together to protect one of the foals, while our dog just wanted to play with him. It hit me all of a sudden, that animals will instinctively protect their animals. All these pain over feeling lost and unprotected came up at once and it was like a slap in the face, it was real!

I was unable to eat, sleep and just perform day to day stuff. Now that this was out there, I was just empty and numb inside. I looked out of the window, not hearing my husband or being aware of what was going on around me. It is like some of the daily functions were just done like following a program, without being conscious of doing them. Minutes seemed like hours and hours like minutes, there was no concept of time. I just did not feel anything and my mind seemed blank. I appeared to be just an empty shell.

My mother reacted pretty much as expected. I was

an ungrateful daughter in her opinion and as long as I was being like this, she wanted nothing to do with me anymore or talk. If I changed and acted like a decent daughter, I was allowed to contact her again.

So, we have not talked for years now and I am just finally starting to feel better. No more taking emotional hurtful things from her or pretending a relationship that was fake from beginning to end. She accused my husband of brain-washing me. And he has his challenges, but it was her that did not like not to have the control anymore.

Since I don`t have her in my life, I was actually able to make progress and I was able to move forward. I am not scared of the phone ringing anymore and I can be who I really am. No more pretending to keep her calm and happy. I can concentrate on what it is that I need to do for my husband and son and also am ok to look after myself.

Of course I still care about my mother and hope she is happy. But from a distant point and whatever there is as relationship, at least is real.

And recently I was able to let go and forgive all the things that were still nagging and hurting. I had to pray lots and over and over for this to happen, as the little girl inside was not ready. But through the strength of the Holy Spirit, I was able to send her a letter, letting her know that I had forgiven her for what went wrong in the past. I still do not call her, as her life partner hangs up on either my husband or me. But you know, that is ok as well. As this way the responsibility does not lie with me. If she truly wanted contact, she could write or call as well. And so finally I can let go and live the life god has intended for me.

It is of course a huge struggle to remember that God is there with us every step of the way. Knowing I am saved and protected sometimes isn`t enough and one still faces days, where it is easier to fall into old, destructive behavior patterns, like not eating or over-eating, drinking, not sleeping, neglecting medication, basically avoiding what the body needs, or even directly doing something to harm ourselves, as a form of punishment. And in some cases to simply still feel something, as a proof one is still alive.

Writing this book has caused some challenging moments. Things I thought were dealt with and forgiven, suddenly left me struggling to cope with daily live again. And yeah, you may be thinking now, this sounds like a repeat and she talked about this already. But that is exactly how it feels. Been there, done that, so why all over again…

I think this is one of the challenges in this healing process, you have to keep doing it and go over things until every part of it is resolved. How tiring! I have people telling me, man you are such a strong women. Your story sounds like real life "Cinderella", or you are

resilient and so on. While I appreciate the encourage-
ment, I often felt like screaming: "I don`t want to be
resilient, or be called strong, I just want this pain to
end and feel what I imagine `normal` feels like"

I also came to a point where I even considered all
this pain to be a blessing, as it made me who I am
today. But on those tough days, I feel more irritated
by everything and the positive angle is much harder to
find. But then I guess I have to be "gentle with myself".
And this is for the most part Shirley talking. At first
I did not even know what it meant. I struggled with
that, as growing up all I knew and was taught that oth-
ers come first and that I had to consider other people
feelings and that you should be there for everyone if
they need you. It gets pretty exhausting, to never really
take yourself as important and always have someone
that needs you, or something of you. Then I finally
clued in to what Jesus had said: "Love your neighbor
like yourself…!"

I lived by highlighting YOUR NEIGHBOUR and
I finally understood that it is supposed to be equal and
LIKE YOURSELF counted just as much. Did I really
misunderstand his teaching? Isn`t the Catholic Church
taking that point of view? Well, it is still something I
am wondering about today. But fact is, if we never con-
sider ourselves and just keep putting out, we will run on
empty and pretty soon have nothing left to give. I don`t
think selfishness is the answer and it is a very fine line.

Of course I will continue to do what God puts on my heart, to the extend that I can give. And I will pray that God will guide me and gives me the strength and energy, as long as it is His will. And to learn that it is ok to be kind and nurturing with oneself. This was probably the second hardest thing for me to learn, or rather still is.

I wish I could just snap my fingers and be done with all this healing and just move forward and be done with old pain, wrong thinking and just always be happy and at peace. Well, maybe not realistic, but with what I have experienced since I walk closer with God, nothing is impossible for Him. But am I willing to open up to that possibility and will I let Him take over? We control our future so much more than we realize, by thinking positive and telling those negative thoughts to go away. Crazy? Mh, maybe so, but I am starting to believe more and more that by handing feelings and myself over to God and start to encourage myself to think positive, I actually attract positive outcomes.

It will certainly be a new challenge from one day to the next. But I have tried the other way for almost 40 years now and it did not get me anywhere I want to be. The last year or so, I have changed things, let God take over and guide me and I seem to slowly make progress. No more meds, but prayer instead. Try to accept that I have hard days where old things need to be allowed to come up and the reality of it accepted. I was not able to or allowed myself to grief. It is high time that little kid inside is taken serious. No one else can replace that and once we can say out loud we are hurting, yes it becomes real. But now I can also take it out and replace it with acceptance, love and understanding. What the abuser or people that allowed it, are not able to give, WE can give to that little child inside. And then give the pain over to our creator and let him heal the wounds and renew us.

Do I Confront

Not sure why it was buried so long in my mind.
It is so very unkind.
I thought I have no right to ask for answers,
as this could possibly hurt others.
Now that I really had to look at the issue…
Those people I had used as the reason for
"Do not disturb"
Have now grown up and live in their own world.

So now I have to decide, do I want this brought
out into the light, or do I go back and hide?

It makes me feel so ashamed and dirty.
Here I am almost into the forties.
Why not just leave it in the dark?
It is so overwhelming and hard.

Even my partner may feel different if he found out.
What if I start to remember it fully?
I am afraid I will not be able to take all of it.
What if they say it was my fault, what made me
to scared to make him stop?
I'm sure I was scared, but is that an excuse?

I was brought up to be a good girl.
Cover your head and don't look at a man.
And here it went much to far.
So how should I feel about myself today and now?
I can't even get a straight thought to put down…

Here Again...

Distress and emptiness is all I feel.
Hanging on just by a threat.
Happiness and laughter seem so far away today.

No energy to live, nor have the strength to die.
You don`t expect yet a goodbye.

They say goodbye is not forever.
But forever seems this pain.

It makes me wonder if there is an everlasting life?
Where is the sense in suffering?
Where is the sense in life, if it only brings you pain...

Excuse or Not?

*Have you ever stopped and thought what
makes a person do all that?
Some say it is the will of god,
then others claim the devil.
He told me I have no choice but
do his evil.*

*Isn`t this a bit convenient, to find
a higher power that can be labelled?
It really takes away the need to
take responsibility for once own deed.*

*If I have caused some pain and hurt,
it was my decision and not God`s.
It really needs to stop,
that people play this game
and bring on so much suffering and shame.*

Facing Up

Torn are my feelings, do not want to choose.
I love them both dearly, am scared I might
end up where one will loose.

Some of the old feelings are getting mixed in.
Things from the past makes the mind go crazy
and go fast. It is hard to decide which comes
from what. The pain takes over and clear
thinking is mixed up.

I don`t want to end up again in the dark…
I have to sit down and write it out,
before of anything I can speak out loud.

I hope by the end there will be not more
pain and hope all this struggling is not in vain.

6

Facing Reality

Ok, I guess instead of hoping, wishing and waiting, it is time now to look at what life realistically is. I have talked to a lot of other people that are aware they are survivors and people that are at some level aware they were sexually abused, but don`t think there is a problem. And I think we all need to deal with past trauma a little different. We are different people with different values, different strength and abilities. There are some people that may only need a little bit of counseling and they seem to cope quite well and live satisfying life`s and look happy and productive. But I have seen a lot more people that find it hard to even find good counseling and even when one finally finds a good match and trust is build, we often have years of work ahead of us and it often seems there is no real improvement. But that only fits, if we measure by society`s standards and only measure success in material values and what kind of success in the type of career one has. I just don`t think those are good standards in any case! Real success and good coping skills will result in a person that has true peace in their heart, is generally happy and has a positive, encouraging outlook on life and beyond. Material belongings, a good career and other types of property are really just an illusion. We cannot take them with us when we go, they don`t bring real and lasting happiness and they lose their value with time or disappear completely.

Which than brings me back to a spiritual relationship with our creator, regardless of what you call it, in my case it is God. Building and trusting in a connection to the divine, is not only what I would consider to be true success in life, but also the ultimate way to heal old and present wounds. I do believe there is a negative energy out there and it will use any means to disconnect us from God, love and hope. Since blinding us with this pain will increase its strength. Prayers and positive thinking however, will weaken negativity. So this is why I believe we have a choice, only we get fooled into thinking we don`t. And what do I have to lose by talking to a God that says He loves me, He will not abandon me and by trusting in Jesus who cared so much about our spiritual well being, that He took on all this suffering and ultimately gave His physical life for us. Again, I am not trying to convince anybody here to choose my believe system. But it is what seems to help me, defines my values and most important to the subject of the book, gives me the strength for wanting to heal!

A few months back, while already working on this book, I was fortunate enough to be baptized again as an adult. It is just something I felt I needed to do for myself and I wanted to openly proclaim that I accept Jesus into my heart.

I will explain in a bit why I bring this up here. There are different levels of courses the local Sexual Assault Centre offers. I had physically completed the second level, but something shut down emotionally, afraid of doing some of the exercises. So I said, I would repeat that course at a later time, only this time not resisting what comes up. I found lots of excuses and years went by. Suddenly beginning of last year I was early for a group session and listened to some relaxing music and prayed. I asked God to help me heal and that I needed His help, since I did not feel strong enough on my own. Coincidence or not, I let you be the judge. That same evening was a new level two group starting, there was room in that group and for a change the timing worked this time. I was stunned, but agreed to come back later again and take this group as I said I would given the opportunity. I just had enough time to go for supper, get a short break and then back for the evening group of AMAC 2 (adults molested as children). Than doubts came up... I got more and more scared of actually facing some of what would no doubt come up. I sat in the new group and it turned out most of the women new each other from the first group. Panic came up and I felt like the outsider again, just like as a child. I had my stuff in hand and was ready to run. Then I closed my eyes for just a moment and to my surprise it felt like Jesus himself was there. Talking to me and telling me that I was ok. I was not alone anymore this time around. He took the hand of the adult woman and than the hand of the little girl inside in His other hand. "You need to join them to heal completely and I will be hear and give you the strength". I felt like falling on my knees and crying. ME, Jesus himself takes the time for me??? I was so humbled, happy and felt like crying at the same time...

If he took the time, how could I let Him down?! I actually made it through and I found it very hard, but I did the exercises. And every time I felt like giving up, I remembered Jesus holding the hand of each part of me, like building the bridge.

Another one during a visualization exercise when we were suppose to imagine going into the woods, taking a big stick and imagine a big boulder that represented all the pain, hurt and anger in us and start beating it with the stick. I stopped myself and hesitated since this seemed like violence to me. But violence was what I was trying to get away from and I struggled and prayed for an answer. I than saw a ball of white light appear and it turned into a vision of Jesus, almost see through, but clearly His image. He stretched out His left hand towards me and the little girl beside me. Somehow without words we knew what He wanted and we put each our hand in His left hand. Than He lifted the right hand and lifted it over the bolder and it started to get smaller, eventually starting to burn, burning up pain, hurt, anger and everything negative related to my past.

From that day on the image of me screaming at the top of my lungs in the forest, bending over forward on my knees, as all my energy goes towards screaming out the pain, started to get less and less. And I shifted to ask Jesus to meet me and help me to shrink this painful feelings again. For the most part my anger is getting less and I feel much more balanced. Writing this book has brought out more unfinished pain and I need to remind myself to ask for help again.

I know He will help, if I only remember to ask for it!

I also like to share here what I had written out as my testimony, since so much of it deals with my painful past.

I grew up with parents that come from the Catholic and a Muslim background. But was fortunate enough to have a strong believing grandmother and a loving, encouraging aunt that also became my baptism witness.

I was baptized as a requirement for my first communion at the age of 9 at a catholic church. Partially because I wanted to, but mostly to be a part of the family and community I was living in at the time. I did believe in Christ already and was deeply moved by the suffering He had gone through for us and felt drawn on some level. Attending church and attending a catholic all girl school. But I did not yet fully understand God`s love for us and did not have a personal relationship. A so called Christian life was more about following rules and procedures, trying to earn God`s favor. Rather than having Christ in my heart. I believed with my mind, but my heart was still empty and searching for truth. Also my life was sometimes complicated by feelings of abandonment from parents, that struggled themselves and a very hurt step-family. I survived sexual and emotional abusive situations that left me thinking I did not deserve anything good, or love. Looking back now, I know that God was already holding me up. I am slowly healing from the pain in the past over the last couple of years. God has send me special people during this time, that *have accepted me for who I am, but always encouraged a relationship with Christ. And people like….. you know who you are…, have made a big difference in finding my way back to God and I am truly thankful for that!*

Than I was blessed to witness what the Holy Spirit can accomplish, if we just keep praying for a person. And I got to see how my husband was transforming from a non-believing, searching person, to a man filled with excitement and love for God. I remember when I listened to someone else`s testimony that was also dealing with an abusive past, I broke down and could not belief God would not spare me this pain. I screamed in my mind and asked God why He allowed this and why He left me alone in such darkness? He did not take long to answer me and said He never left me, but I was shutting Him out. And that He also gave me my "best friend", my husband, so I would not have to face these challenges alone…

On another occasion I was driving and felt like giving up, as everything around me seemed hopeless. I was crying so hard that I had to pull over and while I was telling God I couldn`t take anymore, the car radio that usually did not play, or at least not well, started to clearly play the song: "Don`t give up/You are loved…" by Josh Groban. I knew in my heart without a question, God had chosen to answer me this way and I felt overwhelmed with His love.

There are a lot of things that God has done for me in my life, but I am learning more and more now that these things are blessings from God. He was always there and cared when no one else seemed to. I never fit in anywhere in my life, but God accepts me no matter how different, or broken. It is because Christ suffered and gave His life for me, that I have a chance to truly live. I want to make the best of what God has given me. And I give my life to His teachings and I know He deserves so much more…

Inconvenient Truth

Again… so many years have past.
Seems time does not heal wounds,
but rather does preserve them.
It hides and tricks, making us believe
one is safe. And then comes back and
stares us in the face.

Again… so much has happened.
Some good, some bad, some of it even
makes you sad. Here I am again, with
no where left to turn. Even on the inside,
there is nothing left, but burned.

Again… so much has changed.
But one thing does remain.
I`m broken into a thousand pieces,
only you'd never known.

Struggling…

The more I trust in you O`God,
the more the evil one seeks to destroy me.
He takes away my strength in body,
comes with one challenge after another.

He tries to wear me out, so I will give up.
He almost wins and I feel defeated.
But as long as I believe in you, he can not
complete it!

I give my life, my soul and my all…

In You alone I find hope and fulfillment.
Please do not judge my weaknesses,
for there are many. You have shown me
over and over that you will not abandon me,
like my earthly family.

My Lord, I trust in You and hope to be
worthy of such wonderful and unfailing love

7

Putting the Blame Back and Moving On

It is hard to just stick with one chapter and just match the title, as things are not clearly defined and seem to blend. But I think it comes across that over the last couple of pages, which really is a couple of years of life for me, I have changed. Maybe not what I would call healed. But at the very least open to healing and believing that healing can take place.

I really should not use the word blame I suppose. This is not, nor was this about blaming. It really is about being able to give the past a voice it did not have before, or better, was not allowed to have a voice. It is a way to break the silence that will continue to scream on the inside, if not given a way to be heard. And it is not relevant if this is how anybody else would choose to describe my experiences. This is the point, these are my memories, how I perceive the past. A way for my inner being to express itself. It might sound similar to someone else's story, or not at all. It is not fiction, as what is written here actually happened and it is told how I have felt it.

I am not looking to confront anyone. If so, maybe my own conscious? But really this is about coming to terms with events in the past that took a lot of courage to confront, accept and process. It is an ongoing process and with each new thing learned there comes new opportunity to process more.

I have come from being oblivious to what was haunting me, to slowly realizing a painful reality, to grieving the resulting losses and coming to terms and learning to accept me for being that person, a survivor.

I come from being a shy person that put everyone else's needs before my own. Unable to make decisions for myself, or at the least struggling with decision making. Terrified of being alone and still scared of people coming to see me, or seeing who I am, to being ok to be alone now. Being absolutely untrusting and afraid of being close to someone, out of fear to be hurt by that person again. Trust has been broken by every person I felt close to and that I trusted. But I have learned to forgive and to trust in God instead of people. I am trying now to understand a person, versus taking it on personally. That does not mean a person is not responsible for their actions. But I have a better understanding why someone makes bad choices and out of their guilt and unprocessed pain, hurts a loved one. We are all here to learn, but we can start to help each other, instead of blaming, so everyone ends up being a little better off. Did I deserve to be hurt the way I was while growing up and past that, no. But everyone I look at, was dealing with a tremendous amount of looses and pain themselves. If I keep looking for accusations and continue the hurt and negativity, than negativity wins. Evil can only be stopped with love and forgiveness. So I choose emotional freedom, love and healing.

This viscous cycle needs to be stopped and replaced with positive, nurturing feelings, images and hope. So rather than pointing the finger, I choose to speak up and say what I have a right to. Than let go of it and let God neutralize it and replace it with a sense of accomplishment, understanding and peace. A person that is just starting out with his or her healing journey may call this crazy. And even someone who is doing this longer than I have. But I do believe this is my choice and so I hope this encourages more people to choose freedom from pain and the traumatic past. And that this will truly result into a healed heart and a healed spirit, being capable of having compassion for others, perfect or not.

I have made some bad choices myself and can only hope others will be able to forgive me as well. This is just another way for life to go full circle, where we will be able to help each other, rather than to destroy.

Peace

The world is all fighting.
It makes me so sad.
Why are we just looking for the bad?

We have to start putting our hands and
heads together. Only than can we make
it all better.

This is my wish for today and for forever.
We have to find peace with our neighbor.
All over the world we have to make friends.
And let our hearts join together in songs.

We lift our hearts up to the Lord and
thank Him for what now comes to the world.
We cherish the love and peace for each other.
And see every person as sister and brother.

Being

Being is breathing, to listen, to feel
and to be aware of every presence
around you.
It`s being still, lost in the moment and thereby timeless.

No today, or past, or tomorrow.
No plans for what needs to be done.

Just breathing and listening and being now.
No wars, no fighting. A pleasant place.
No complains of loved once, no settling of scores.

Just breathing and listening and being now.

To feel the lungs fill up with air.
To feel the muscle tone relax.
To sense your body taking up his space
without time.

Just breathing and listening and being now…

God`s Tree

I am like a tree in Jesus` garden.
The seed was dropped so many years ago,
but the soil was burned and it wasn`t watered.
Now that the seed was washed into the deeper,
rich and nourishing soil, the young, vulnerable
seedling is starting to sprout.
God waters it now every day with truth and
knowledge, so that it is slowly growing into
a tree.
A fresh green new leaf and it ever so stretches
towards the sun. It is still vulnerable, but Jesus
has His protecting shield around me.
And I grow slowly in His blessing.
Bigger, stronger and shaped by His will.
Hopefully I will be a mighty oak tree at the end
of times, that will give shelter and refuge to others
still looking to find Him…

After all this work I have to say, I am certainly not a professional writer. And never in my wildest dreams did I ever expect to write a book. But I have to say I am very grateful for this opportunity. It was very hard at times, but also helped to really having to look at some things, that are easier to ignore than to address. It helped me to understand myself better. Reading this as if it was another person, I could see why there are struggles. I just hope as scary as it is to put my life experiences and feelings out there, for everyone to see in black in white. It will help at least some of them, to realize what they are going through, should not isolate them. It has happened to others as well and yes, there is hope to get past the hurt. The memories will stay, but how one reacts to them and how they interfere with life, love and other relationships and most of all how we feel about ourselves can be changed!

Aside from reaching the next step in my journey to become a happier, healthier person, it gives me the opportunity to communicate something I still find hard to say verbally. Just by telling the story, it feels like for the first time that little girl inside has been given a voice and does no longer have to stay silent. I am finally getting past the fear of being judged. Not completely, as it is an ongoing process. For that reason it is not written under my legal name, but under the name that the "little girl" on the inside carried, when this happened to her. A lot of it was written under *A Wondering Soul*, and it is still how I identify the traumatized part of me. But this is also about not hiding the truth any longer and to finally let the girl inside speak. I thought about it a lot and discussed this with friends and while I still have poems out under "A Wondering Soul", this is about a real story, told by a real person.

The names I have been called during my life have changed more than once, but this is who I always was and will continue till my time here is up. It does not change facts in my life, or how I relate to them.

I just like to encourage others to take some time for themselves, to sit down and write to yourself, to God, or however you need to address this to. And hopefully it will be as helpful and healing as it was for me. And may God bless you on your journey!

Nurturing Rain

The rain it falls and takes the pain. It cools the heat and washes off, what burns and stings us to the core. I stand and let it happen. It cleanses and creates life, where only pain and sorrow would have stained tomorrow.

The rain it falls and creates a southing sound. Drowns out the sound of hurt. It washes of the dirt and is able to let flowers grow, where once the dirty places were. The flower feeds the butterfly, who is a symbol of new life!

From Burning Wound to Healing Light...

A little child is fragile yet. It needs to trust, needs nurturing and love. The people closest are like a touch in the development of spirit and mind.

Yet sometimes, sadly all to often, those touches we receive in early life are really not so very kind.
The way it`s touched it causes damage. Resulting in a burning wound. These burning wounds contain the pain and broken trust combined. They often stay for lot`s of years.
Start weeping, draining, flaring up when touched upon again. They harden, toughened up by life and slowly will be filled with scars. So thick, it won`t feel a gentle touch, meant well by someone that is kind.

Than comes the divine. It reaches through the thickest scar, softens each scar with acceptance and with love. He starts to heal one spot at a time. Slowly transforming this body of scars into wounds transformed to light.
The light shines so bright and beautiful and kind to the eye. Each light of unconditional love now shines where once a scar had been.

8

After Writing This Book

As I finish these last pages, I come to realize how blessed I am. Not just for surviving situations I have been through. But for this chance to freely share so much about what I feel, my values and what I believe. It is a bit scary to put such personal experiences out there. But over the last little while, already sharing so much of what I have been allowed to write, it came through that it engages people and brings out their experiences, which lead to some very insightful discussions. It touched some women in a very personal way, as it can trigger their memory and I was surprised how similar some of it sounded. But every time it left me, and I think others, with a sense of a deeper understanding and just maybe a bit of healing.

I enjoyed what reading this to others can bring out in people and the sharing connected us on a very personal level. I love and welcome the questions this might raise. As challenging each other to think things through and so moving forward and learning, is a wonderful gift we have been given by our creator. And I am still in awe, that God thought of me worthy enough to complete a project like this. It disproves also something my mother used to say when she was trying to get me to do something: "You never finish what you start…". Well looking back on that, I finished this, despite enormous difficulties. And not only this project, but also a lot of other accomplishments in my life. But none would have been successful without God guiding and providing every step of the way.

Because this material can be very sensitive for a person with similar experiences, regardless of how much you are aware of it or not. I don`t want to leave you on your own and so tried to leave you with a bit of info on where to go to get help and suggested some other readings and so hope to not leave struggling.

I will also try to have a contact option through the books website, since there is sometimes a special connection that gets made reading something so personal. But if this leaves you overwhelmed and struggling, please first of all remember to keep breathing. Remind yourself to stay in the moment and maybe write down what is coming up. There is good counseling available, it just sometimes takes a bit of searching to make the right connections.

AFTER WRITING THIS BOOK

But the most important advice I feel I need to share is, that God is already there with you right in this moment. We often are to scared to admit it to ourselves and even more to others. But deep inside of you, you can trust your loving creator and talk to Him. He will hear you and guide you. His love is unfailing and crosses any boundary. There is nothing He can not heal and make whole again. Even as broken as we often feel and think we do not even deserve healing. Every life was created by Him and is precious. It was not that He just allowed this to happen to us, but He gives us all free will and sometimes we all make the wrong choices. And He cries with us when we are crying. But He will also restore us, if we only invite Him in, allowing Him to heal.

I know I am an example of His strength, but there are many more out there. Coming together in His love, will heal suffering and fear.

Please be assured that I will include you in my prayers. As this book was not done for my benefit, but in hopes of helping others to get hope and to glorify His work in me.

Thank you for taking the time to read this book. And just maybe this can help a little in creating awareness, for the large amount of women in shelters or in our neighborhoods, that can use some support or just a kind word of encouragement.

If only one person will get enough courage to turn to God and ask for His help and love, the time I invested in this book was more than worse my time. Jesus himself says: "I am with you always…"

Appendix
Where Help Can Be Found…

Books

"Beyond our control"   *by Leila Rae Sommerfeld*

"If you tell it would kill you mother"   *by Ardith Trudzik*

"Just Breath – Hope Beyond Hurt"   *by Teresa Rilling*

"Prayers that Heal the Heart"   *by Mark & Patti Virkler*

"I was the Devil`s Egg"   *by Robert J. Kuglin*

Websites

Alberta Association of Sexual Assault Centres
www.aasac.ca

Kawartha Sexual Assault Centre
www.kawarthwsexualassaultcentre.com

Recovery Canada – the Wellness Network
www.vansondesign.com/RecoverCanada/SexualAbuse/
Library

The Support Network
www.thesupportnetwork.com

Alberta Council of Women`s Shelters
www.acws.ca

Shelternet – Canada wide Shelter List
www.shelternet.ca

CPSIA information can be obtained at www.ICGtesting.com
Printed in the USA
LVOW102118101212

310987LV00004B/17/P